VIKING
Published by the Penguin Group
Penguin Books USA Inc., 375 Hudson Street, New York, New York 10014, U.S.A.
Penguin Books Ltd, 27 Wrights Lane, London W8 5TZ, England
Penguin Books Australia Ltd, Ringwood, Victoria, Australia
Penguin Books Canada Ltd, 10 Alcorn Avenue, Toronto, Ontario, Canada M4V 3B2
Penguin Books (N.Z.) Ltd, 182-190 Wairau Road, Auckland 10, New Zealand

Penguin Books Ltd, Registered Offices: Harmondsworth, Middlesex, England

First published in Great Britain by William Heinemann Ltd,
an imprint of Reed Children's Books, 1993
First published in the United States of America by Viking,
a division of Penguin Books USA Inc., 1994

1 3 5 7 9 10 8 6 4 2

Copyright © Catherine and Laurence Anholt, 1993
All rights reserved
Library of Congress Catalog Card Number: 93–60905
ISBN 0–670–85261–9

Printed in Hong Kong

Catherine and Laurence Anholt

ONE, TWO, THREE,
COUNT WITH
ME

VIKING

One, two, three,
Count with me,
Counting everything we see.

2 eyes

1 nose

10 fingers

1 tummy

2 legs

10 toes

Let's count together.

Can you count from one to ten
Round the park and back again ?

6

7

8

9

10

Count with me in the garden...

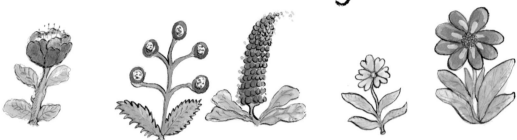

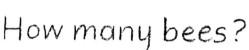

How many flowers?

How many bees?

How many butterflies?

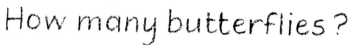

How many trees?

How many clothes are hanging out to dry?

How many kites are flying in the sky?

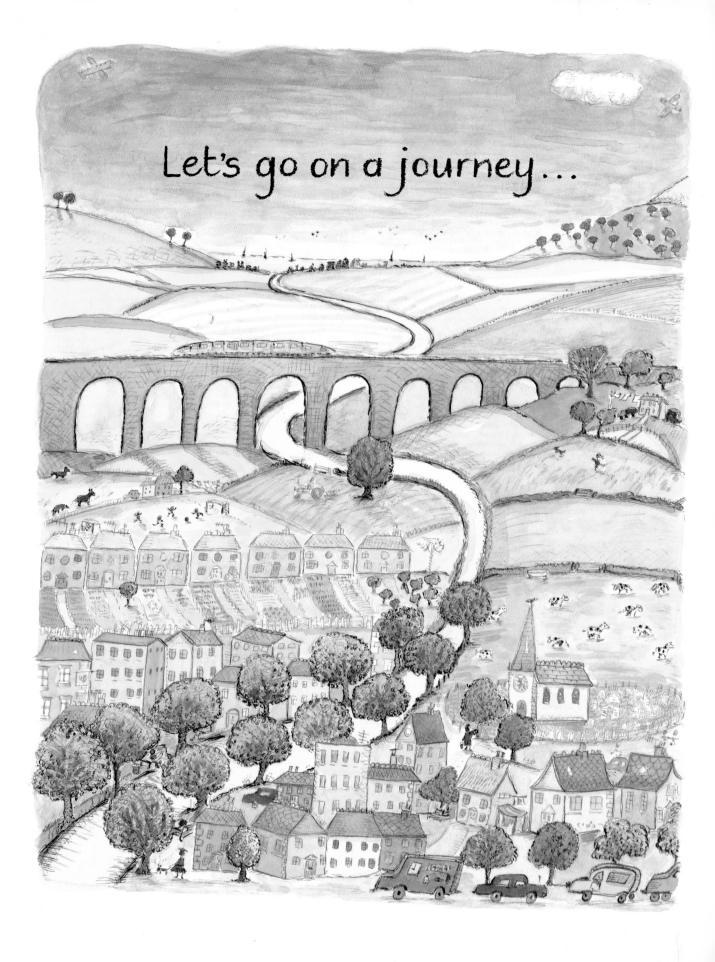

Let's go on a journey...

counting bikes,

counting cars,

counting trains,

counting trucks,

counting boats,

counting planes.

We can count animals...

1 mouse in a house,

2 bears on a chair,

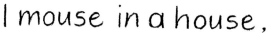

3 goats in a boat,

4 foxes in boxes,

5 kittens in mittens,

6 owls with towels,

7 moles in holes,

8 rats in hats,

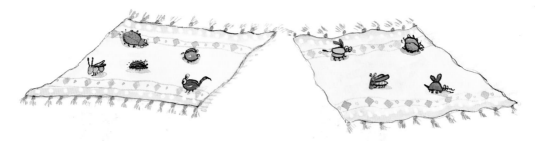

9 bugs on rugs,

10 sheep asleep.

The farmer says it isn't hard
To count the animals in the yard –
How many chickens pecking on the path?
How many ducklings going for their bath?
How many cows are waiting to be fed?
How many piglets are hiding in the shed?

I like counting every day.
Let's count the children as they play.

Monday

Tuesday

Wednesday

Thursday

Friday

Saturday

Sunday

How many days in the week?

We can count BIG things...

and LITTLE things too...

birds   blocks   bubbles   beads

stones   shells   stamps   seeds

raisins   ribbons   rings   rice

money   marbles   moths   mice

pins   pens   paints   peas

fruit   freckles   flowers   fleas

badges   bells   bears   bags

fish   flies   fairies   flags

Counting colors is fun...

One white clown
all by herself,

Two brown bears
on a purple shelf,

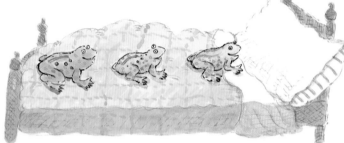

Three green frogs on an orange bed,

Four big trucks, all painted red,

Five black spiders, six pink balloons,

Seven yellow teacups with seven yellow spoons,

Eight blue dolls and nine gold rings,

Ten is a box full of colorful things.

Now we can count anything!

10 big shoes for 10 big feet,

20 puppies, aren't they sweet!

100 lovely things to eat, and ...

a million stars above my street.